[Translating *Requiem*]

[Translating *Requiem*]

poems and translation by
Hoyt Jacobs

Winner of the Loose Translation Prize

HL&QC
Loose Translations Prize

Hanging Loose Press
Brooklyn, New York

Copyright © 2015 by William Jacobs and Susan Posey

Published by Hanging Loose Press, 231 Wyckoff Street, Brooklyn, New York 11217-2208. All rights reserved. No part of this book may be reproduced without the publisher's written permission, except for brief quotations in reviews.

www.hangingloosepress.com

Printed in the United States of America
10 9 8 7 6 5 4 3 2 1

Hanging Loose Press thanks the Literature Program of the New York State Council on the Arts for a grant in support of the publication of this book.

Cover design: Marie Carter

Cover art: *The Elevated*, by Margaret Lowengrund, ca. 1935. Lithograph 11 3/8" x 12 3/4". Gift of Audrey McMahon, PO15, collection of The Godwin-Ternbach Museum, Queens College.

ISBN 978-1-934909-88-1

Library of Congress cataologing-in-publication available on request.

This is the fourth winner of the Loose Translation Prize, co-sponsored by Queens College–City University of New York and Hanging Loose Press. The competition is open to students and recent graduates of the MFA program at Queens.

The editors of this collection, Kimiko Hahn and Rajiv Mohabir, extend their thanks to Bill Jacobs and Susan Posey, Hoyt's parents, and to all of Hoyt's friends, classmates, professors, and fellow cyclists.

CONTENTS

Foreword	11
Introduction	13
Yamanaka, after Basho	19
Two Ghost Stories: The Stolen Liver & Ellipsis	20
Cepo	24
"Anything But an Apple" *after a story by Olga Ardova*	25
Another Ghost Story	26
Motor Lodge	27
Postcards	29
Stillness in the Park	31
A Question of Metaphoric Death	32
The Haff-Man	33
Lonely	40
Misinterpreting 'Field Work'	41
Two Can't Tell the Difference Poems	45
By a Fish	46
The city cascading down; people churning like stones in a plunge pool; tall buildings with glass facades.	47
Train	49
Liminal Poem: Between Nut and Tree	50
REQUIEM by Anna Akhmatova, *translated from the Russian with Olga Adorva*	51
Instead of a Preface	52
Dedication	53
Prologue	54
Epilogue	64
Шестое чувство, *a translation of Percy Bysshe Shelley's* "Ozymandias" *from English into Russian*	67
Ozymandias, *a "Google Translation" of Percy Bysshe Shelley's* "Ozymandias" *from English to Russian*	68
The Sixth Sense, by Nicolay Gumilev, *translated from the Russian with Olga Adorva*	69
Giraffe, by Nicolay Gumilev, *translated from the Russian with Olga Adorva*	70
Two Jealousy Poems	71
Acknowledgments	73

… Round the decay

Of that colossal wreck, boundless and bare

The lone and level sands stretch far away.

Percy Bysshe Shelley

Foreword

What a name. *Hoyt*. The name of a street and subway stop. A memorable name, at once castle and holler.

I am one of two editors of this collection because Hoyt Jacobs was fatally hit by a truck while riding his bicycle on January 17th. He was thirty-six and on his way to a poetry reading. His death made the news because he was "the first NYC cyclist to die in 2015." As I type this revised foreword, we are still in 2015. I am still in that disbelief that accidents perpetrate.

I knew Hoyt as his instructor and thesis advisor. Certainly that may seem scarcely knowing him, but given how his poetry and translations resonate, how he developed that resonance, it is knowing him plenty. And of course, whether in workshop, office, or corridor, I regarded him as the quintessential trickster.

You will find in his work an ardent engagement with language. Hear it. Feel the blast or vibrations. And the quiet—a quiet that may be a sigh, a grin, or a moment of *what-the—?*

What else did I know of him? His missing front tooth. His inappropriate garb in the copy room. His pissing off classmates—*and* absolutely delighting them. Above all, I knew a resolve. *Others* will speak of this resolve, this doggedness. And from the outpouring of despair at his sudden death, I know there will be many chances to speak of him, on behalf of him, and, *Hoyt, here's to you—*

Kimiko Hahn
Flushing, Queens

Poetry Between Translation and the Original: an Introduction to [Translating *Requiem*]

Once the initial shock of Hoyt's death calmed, I emailed the Queens College MFA thread that director Nicole Cooley uses to keep students and alumnae updated. I wanted to know how many of us saved Hoyt's work on our computers. I never did delete his poems—not for any sentimental reason, but because I believed in Hoyt's work.

Hoyt and I began the MFA program together at Queens College. He strode into workshop, messenger bag slung across one shoulder, sweaty from walking from the Q64 bus stop. The first poem that Hoyt workshopped in class appears in this posthumous collection: "Stillness in the Park" is imagistic, spare, deadly.

Editing this collection was a task that Kimiko and I have done, wanting to preserve as much of Hoyt's work as we could. We faced one major task: how to edit a collection of poems and translations into a cohesive manuscript that displays Hoyt's strengths as a poet? It was upon reading the poems in Hoyt's MFA thesis, chillingly entitled "Requiem," that we discovered the dialogue between his translations and his poetry.

Because we were the ones to decide on the title, we began with "Requiem" from his thesis. But the word did not convey the various dimensions of his work here so we added "Translating." By bracketing "Translating *Requiem*," we are acknowledging that this was a posthumous decision *and* one that we feel fully exemplifies Hoyt's experimentation with translation and creation: something new sprung of something old. The title itself serves as indication of the aesthetic and poetic at stake. Indeed Hoyt ponders the distance between influence, assimilation, originality, and plagiarism in his poem "What We Share (or, Learning to Translate) (Or, I am Ripping You off)." He writes,

> Before walking home I sit in the pews of a Gothic Revival church reading "The Garden of Forking Paths." I return to my apartment and attempt to recreate the story. This does not work. When I remember myself remembering the church, I am bathed

13

in the resolving light of stained glass windows and scaffolding.
My footsteps echo long after I'm seated. I would prefer the use
of a better memory. That is to say, one of my own invention.

It is from this poem that the organizing principle of this book emerged: trying to create something new, something of Hoyt's "own invention" that engages his poetic influences and obsessions. We learn a little about his own process of writing—that it is an act of translation, or borrowing from what moves him as a reader.

There is a poetic Hoyt experiments with—something syncretic and novel. Placing translations alongside Hoyt's poems show just how it takes a whole poet to translate a whole poem. Whatever his process of working with the "raw" texts and wringing the rough translations into poems; the poems that spring up show a continuity of a young poet studying at the feet of a master. It is our hope that this collection illustrates Hoyt's experimentation with gravity. Here, Kimiko and I hasten to acknowledge Olga Ardova's fluency in Russian as part of Hoyt's process.

The book starts with original poems by Hoyt that set the tone and foreground the relationship between translation and Hoyt's poetry. He invokes Basho at the start of this journey—a template for the presence and absence that haunts Hoyt's work. This presence and absence is at once of the poet/translator and as the original poet that Hoyt translates. Who ghosts these poems? The answer can be unearthed through the interplay between sections.

Akhmatova's poetry, as presented here, serves as a template of bleakness that Hoyt aspired to achieve with his own writing. The prose piece "The Haff-Man," too, exposes this, though the speaker's does not survive the same brand of Akhmatova's Stalinist terror. There is a forgetting, an erasure of presence that Akhmatova writes,

> I want to call out to them, each by name,
> but the list that names them was stolen.

as she alone bears witness to the disappearance of the people around her. If we don't remember and recall the names of those passed, do they disappear?

Rather than deal fully in death as disappearance, Hoyt migrates the poetic to reflect an interior terror: being rendered invisible to those around him. Despite the Haff-man's brief celebrity of such unusual suffering, Hoyt writes that upon the voyeurs

> a silence that could not be marred by car horns or approaching sirens or the howls of dogs would descend vertigolike upon them.
>
> and the Haff-man would be but memory.

But all is not erasure and destitution in these pages. The theme of love is also threaded throughout this collection like a red ribbon beginning with "CEPO," into "The Sixth Sense." This shows continuity between Hoyt and his translations from the Russian as something foundational and moving.

As an envoi, Hoyt's collection ends with "Two Jealousy Poems" as a way to cycle back into the space between borrowing from his favorite poetry in order to create something in dialogue with the original.

The collection ends with a prayer, a closure that reflects Hoyt's poetry and his contribution to the American poetic landscape. His last words chill as they contemplate the death of the poet Craig Arnold, caught forever in a volcano, disappeared and petrified the same. Hoyt's words could be my own when he says,

> Today   I miss you terribly.

Rajiv Mohabir
July 2015

[Translating *Requiem*]

Yamanaka

after Basho

Breathless. A flower,
and the valley's volcanic
water, not chosen.

Two Ghost Stories

adapted from the folklore of Russia, Poland & Germany

I

The Stolen Liver

They lived outside a small town, surrounded by forest and river. She needed liver: She could not live without it. Her husband, a soldier, could not live without her. So he went in search of her need. He wandered the town; but no butcher had liver to sell. Distraught, the man found comfort in a barroom's spectral light.

Stumbling home through the woods, he met a hunter decorated with bone, whose voice rattled when he spoke: *Go to the forest's center where the bodies of convicted men hang from spruces. Cut the newest corpse down and take his liver, as you would his life –in haste—for the dead in this forest cherish what little they might call their own.*

The drunken man did just that. He presented the liver to his wife, then slept.

…While he slept, she ate it. Soon a white figure appeared at the table.

What happened to your skin? The wife asked.

The Ravens tore it from my flesh, they filled their bellies, they flew away.

And what happened to your ears?

The Ravens tore them from my deaf skull, they filled their bellies, they flew away.

And what happened to your eyes?

The Ravens tore them from my blind face, they filled their bellies, they flew away.

And what happened to your liver?

There was the steady wind outside, and beyond that, a gentle river, shimmering in the moonlight, but there was no reply.

The husband slept uneasily, dreaming of war and the hunt. Though, as in all drunken sleep, he would not remember those dreams in the morning.

II

Ellipsis

A father and son enlist that winter. Falling
snow and ash. Boot tracks like angular brick-
work, then easy hills. Then, sheets of pure white.

The air fills with smoke, the sky above
their home is mortar and fire; near and far,
the threshold of battle is a swift river

cutting into ground, as animal scent
swirls from the center of a new wind.
Before it congeals to brittle rust,

before it soaks through and stains the snow,
blood must pass through uniform. It runs silent
along its path, breathing the air between

skin and cloth. The father dies. The son
also dies. Their phantoms meet on the forest
road, speechless. From the trees above,

an owl's call reaches a vole. And so too
the men find one another in the progress
of a perfect past, the way all ghosts search

for home. The way of fathers and sons:
shadows without edges, new as dawn,
and as old and unspoken

as words can be. … Between
the trees, two white animals:
a tragic moon, back turned

to the night sky, and a snowshoe hare,
frozen in the whiteness of a white clearing
halved by snowmelt creek.

CEPO

She speaks, and I translate: the fruit she could and could
not have— Her child hands turning that first apple in Red Square,

while Russian blackbirds circle like silent words in the sky.
She tries to catch them, as she falls back to the snowy ground.

Small arms and legs begin to craft an angel.
The child asks why we are born human, not understanding

that people must deliver other people. *Why not a hedgehog?*
Why not a puppy? And I ask the woman before me if her memories

are like my own reimagined American moments:
apparitions, viscid in black and white.

Or does vibrant dream reach her lips like a foregone taste?
The girl-child rolls away, leaving us with what she became.

Then, from the achromatic whiteness, our indentured
angel pivots on shadow-feet, into air. *Wonderful.* I wonder,

what tones gather first in the cup of these make-believe
wings, and slip, barely noticed, through grown hands—

And she tells me, in English, without thinking twice.

"Anything but an Apple"

after a story by Olga Ardova

Anything but an apple. You could always have an apple. Other fruits were multicolored jewels betraying everything I knew about daily life. Their rarity in those ancient summer months; brightness and colors almost blinding in the gray din of Moscow twilights.

There were apartments and stores; leering skyscrapers and squat tenements. There were trains to run my family on errands. There were streets shooting across and through, lines that moved in and out of the capitol city. In or out, yet always deeper into Russian forests.

…Then I saw the melocoton and understood we were in a different place.

Peaches were a crowning jewel, eagerly awaited. The sting of prickly hairs on my chin brought glorious nectar. A price had to be paid. A price always had to be paid. But not here. Not in this new, soft, forgiving place of infinite peaches--bald peaches. And no food lines.

That strange border crossing. Stepping over the invisible division built of handsome guards in clean uniforms and barbed wire. Soldiers standing with guns, watching us lugging large sacks of *most important things* never to be of use again.

I recall wrestling the train for control of my body; the light touch of morning sun on my face, so much like my mother's face, asleep in the seat before me. So much like my father's face, back in Russia. I recall whistles and the rustle of luggage and the sudden movement of my feet.

I recall sweet juice dripping even after the last piece of flesh slid to my stomach.

Another Ghost Story

Katie slams the door for the fifteenth time
she hides in the bathroom, then in the crevice
between the bed and the wall, and I try
to straighten my ruined back, wishing
she'd share the good dope she's got
hidden somewhere.

In the shower she giggles, her piss
running down my leg; at the store she farts
on strangers (and you know, I can't quite allow
them to leave. Oh, how they've shopped)
while I steal breakfast for the dog
--the dog that once bristled and growled
at an empty corner, while Katie said:
                    "There must be a ghost waiting there."

At night she fucks me with a needle's shiver:
warm violence and vomit on the floor;
fragile static electricity dancing on eyelid rims:
vascular purple threads beating desire away.
The dog staring from the bed above us,
                    like we're crazy.

And you just know that that dog's forgotten
how Katie once held me when the ghosts
of that room were too close for words to chase
away… while the weeks and months recycled
and wrecked themselves in circles against the floor
--a floor where I'd bet a stain still holds,
defiant and desperately proud, underneath
                    a stranger's new carpet.

What We Share (or, Learning to Translate) (Or, I Am Ripping You Off)

One about Reading Kafka:

Before walking home I sit in the pews of a Gothic Revival church reading "The Garden of Forking Paths." I return to my apartment and attempt to recreate the story. This does not work. When I remember myself remembering the church, I am bathed in the resolving light of stained glass windows and scaffolding. My footsteps echo long after I'm seated. I would prefer the use of a better memory. That is to say, one of my own invention.

Injection:

A boy enters the water-closet carrying a guitar and does not come out for some time. A sound that might be music, but could also be moaning, is apparent. The people in line begin discussing what might be going on inside the room they are outside of. An employee mentions that people sometimes overdose in it. I think that the boy thinks, *shooting heroin feels like holding the acoustic chamber of an instrument: pure space, no wood.* The sound stops.

Duality:

A conservative and a liberal discuss life. Illegal drugs come up. The first says drugs are about control since drugs are a fraction of everything and everything is about control. The second says they are about distraction from the constant becoming that is life. I realize that I can't tell one speaker from the other, since they are both coming from the same place. I choose to believe this is a joining of past and future, but right now there is no certainty of either.

Motor Lodge

red cobweb   varicose scaffolding
her sleepless   night in soft corners
rises sienna iris   from her milky eyes

a stranger's blue   sheets smooth in
the wake of her   reedy hand and
rustle gently   on a cache of wind

Postcards

Idaho:

In the little garden below the window.
Springtime. My fingers loose on the trowel
handle. Like all southern boys
I take after my mother. Did I ever tell you
she had a green thumb? Or that, like her,
I am often sad.

New York:

You are waiting in our hotel room. I am on the subway
holding the wild flowers I bought for you: An apology.
Striated purples fading to white. Centers of black.
Centers that send stalks down into potted earth.
Airships lowering their tethers
to an outstretched hand.

From an airplane:

What else is there, outside of remembering?
Family and lovers. There is no photo album
to hold you. No record that will not evaporate
like jet stream. Blessed forgetfulness.
I write to you everyday. I wait
for you to write back.

Idaho:

It gets cold in the winter. Jet wings ice.
The garden must be covered before I leave
--a blanket I pin to cold earth with a motherly hand.
But they are not hands. They are clumsy chisels, mallets,
or hooks best suited to split wood. I use them to haul heavy
things through the snow. Dead trees to keep you warm.
To keep you, I must keep you warm.

In the window above the garden:

You have artist's hands. There is a canvas by the door:
a painting of swallows you cannot seem to finish.
There is always some excuse. Today the cold is cramping
your arm. So I hold the brush. I forge the curve of your name.
Standing back to look, you hold your hands out
like a frame. Outside, the snow falls away.

Stillness in the Park

A clean bill of health,
blue sky cut by kites.
Steady, dull traffic,
children like the tinkling
of cafe glasses. Mute
grass sprung beneath
the blanket. The faint
drumming of ants
from cuff to collar
and through the easy
hair behind my ear.
A clean bill of health.
Eddies of breath. Steady,
dull traffic. Tinkling.
Blue sky. Mute grass.

A Question of Metaphoric Death

Before walking home I sit in the pews of a Gothic Revival church reading "The Garden of Forking Paths." I return to my apartment and attempt to recreate the story. This does not work. When I remember myself remembering the church, I am bathed in the resolving light of stained glass windows and scaffolding. My footsteps echo long after I'm seated. I would prefer the use of a better memory. That is to say, one of my own invention.

With a mirror or two I can view the two-headed dog falling down my back. No: it is two dogs engaged in violent birth. The image was implanted by a man many consider France's innovational tattoo artist. For its first year in my skin, it was like nothing on earth. Later I discovered pictures of other two-headed dog tattoos, in a similar vein. Then I learned of the artist's influences. Now my back is the vibrating center of derivation. Now I would get tattooed by anyone. This is the quiddity of it.

Until I knew what a *faux pas* was, I wore bands' tee-shirts to their shows.

Soccer is a game I know precious little about. A man on the train says players must often circumnavigate the goal to score. One assumes he is talking about soccer.

A boy enters the water closet carrying a guitar and does not come out for some time. A sound that might be music, but could also be moaning, is apparent. The people in line begin discussing what might be going on inside the room they are outside of. An employee mentions that people sometimes overdose in it. I think that the boy thinks, *shooting heroin feels like holding the acoustic chamber of an instrument: pure space, no wood*. The sound stops.

The Haff-Man

The man smoking by the gas station wasn't really whole. He was half a man. And not charmingly so: he wasn't half-goat or half-horse or otherwise magical in any innocuous way. Nor was he, or had he been, a hermaphrodite, as far as anyone could tell. He wasn't even a man-child, or some other metaphorical Halfling. And he certainly hadn't been truncated by accident or war. It was hard to explain. He was simply floating there, a smoky haze hovering around his midsection, wearing a sign that read: *haff man. evaperating sinse morning. please Help.*

It was a lovely hustle-bustle summer afternoon. People crowded the streets going this way and that while the man smoldered passively, large black droplets occasionally falling where his legs once were. A spleen-yellow vapor was streaming from his unseen bowels; it licked the front of his shirt before mysteriously disappearing like the first traces of smoke curling from an oven. The occasional breeze hinted at the alien penis of his spinal column swinging metronomically below a nylon rope-belt. In a gloved hand he held a dented tincan matter-of-factly while his eyes scanned the surrounding area with myopic interest.

No one would give him a dime, of course. Most passed him by, averting their eyes out of habit. Someone occasionally took his welfare upon themselves, but they were quickly run off by the wisps of vaporous flesh caressing his change-cup. His smoking torso turned from mucus yellow, to swirling pink and brown, and back again, as the parking lot steadily filled with people. Already there were more than twenty men and women and children there of all races and creeds; they milled at the edge of the pumps, and exchanged redundant observations about the scene with the occasional religious pronouncement treated as equal currency.

The man was floating just to the right of the gas station door and it was affecting business. The owner tried to get rid of him, but found the broom he typically used to shoo the homeless away suddenly ineffectual. The proprietor sighed indiscreetly and set about beating the disappearing man about the head and shoulders with the broom, cursing at him until the words no longer meant anything. But he simply bobbed back and forth like a balloon tethered closely to the wall by invisible yarn. "Maybe we should try a leaf blower", the new hire remarked.

It took four calls to the police department to get any cops to show. When they did finally arrive, their laughter and coffee were quickly dropped and replaced with pistols. Though the haff-man had no discernable weapon, they instinctively used their car doors as shields. Not knowing what else to say, the senior officer bellowed, in his most practiced tone, "You There! Stop Evaporating!" But it was no use. The man didn't seem to notice them at all. He bobbed in the air with the resigned patience of a lone shipwreck survivor waiting hopelessly for someone—anyone— to rescue him. After standing with their guns trained on the man for five minutes the cops looked at each other, shrugged their shoulders and took to crowd control. As he stepped back from the police car, the rookie fumbled his gun in the air. It landed explosively on the ground, but the crowd hardly noticed the shot, so accustomed were they to the antics of the police: The disappearing man seemed much less like something they had seen on television; he was more like the feeling it gave you after a few hours. Unaware of his new cult-status, the man by the gas station wall continued to shake his empty cup from time to time, his head moving slowly back and forth like a drunk trying to cross the street, though by now there was no one within twenty feet of him.

Strange things happened all the time, but no could remember seeing anyone evaporate before. Floodlights were set up. The crowd tripled in size and a barricade was erected. The local Fox affiliate streamed their footage directly to every major market in the country. Pundits debated the possible effect of strong winds and the local meteorologist found himself in high demand for the first time in his ten-year career. Google collapsed under the strain of the haff-man's hits. Small children emailed their neglected grandparents to tell them the news; grandparents in nursing homes heard the wild rumors and went back to bed, and had new nightmares for the first time in years. Neighbors who had never before spoken discussed every detail through their windows. The mayor's recent scandal was forgotten by everyone, including his wife and mistress. Every bar in town erupted with spontaneous cheers.

In a little under an hour the vaporous man would have nothing more than a head, his face hovering in the air above the sidewalk as the skin of his cheeks turned up like burnt paper toward a darkened sky. Then the crowd would turn as one toward him and a silence that could not be marred by car horns or approaching sirens or the howls of dogs would descend vertigolike upon them. And the man's eyes would roll back into his head as the fluid in them bubbled and steamed until nothing remained but a wrinkled forehead and wisps of finger-combed hair on the hovering crown of his skull.

And then, as though finally caught by the wind, there would be nothing more of him.

But for the moment he shook his cup, occasionally sniffing at the air and nodding blankly to himself as if resigned to, if nothing else, gauging his dissipation rate by smell. With his free hand, he scratched his naked scalp absentmindedly. Under the floodlight's scrutiny his eyes reflected the small tin cup shining in his hand, and nothing else.

Lonely

Propped against the wall
that cradles the bed,
reading Yeats until the tangled
tingling words have shivered
their chance moment away &
my arms gone numb, I listen
to the cats of Bushwick
high on their windowsills.

High on their fire escapes:
they are singing the song
of raping one another.

High on their rooftops. Buried
in each other. And above it all

the moon.

Misinterpreting 'Field Work'

I

Young couple on the bus
holding each other's chins,
nibbling away like captive
squirrels, both believing
they've got a nut.
I can't decide
who'll be eaten
by the end
of the night.
So I watch
from the corner
of my eye until their dovetailed
hands strain,
and the quiver
of their
matching
clothes and haircuts
infuriate me.

II

Oh, but I like *you* so much
and in a way I should
probably question
more often. Particularly
when you pull in
the dense white word
balloon of cigarette smoke
floating latent on your lips,

with your simple
melody—that sharp
sucking sound
you make.
Lungfish. Hold your breath
to your heart's content;
blow it thin and pale
into space. Look at me
with your cold lips pursed.
Throw it smoldering to the ground.

III

Not habit. Not comfort.
Not the bones of wild animals
you gnaw in your primitive way.
But something that will not stop
rides lit buses down narrow
streets, pouring white.
 Narrow. Razor. Definition.

IV

Pull the coated chain
and choose a direction.
El train rattling above,
playful Mexicans pass
kicking each other in turn,
umber and energized.
They are distant farmers sent
in service to things I chew.
Static wake, free and over
generous. You and I
and the necessity of completing
a current. Hot breath in cold air.
In the neon glow of a tattoo
parlor, I stoop to tie my shoe.

Two Can't Tell the Difference Poems:

Smoking Cigarettes in the Dark

White light
fill my lungs
transform me
and I will try
again
to transform you

I love drugs

Well, drugs and falling in love
and there isn't a better drug
than love. Except drugs,
which is another thing I love.

By a Fish

I am a thing that moves under water.
That is all you need know.
Like you, I breathe. I move forward
and backward. And that is just the tip
of the tugboat. I am your metaphor
and in that, I am as misunderstood
as you are to yourself.

I look up into your world of things
that spill and stain in imitation
of permanence, where land tethers
even the winged things in the end.
And it is as empty to my eyes
as your imagined heavens.

I move through my world,
and the darkness pressures
me to glow. And the light
on my belly is in imitation
of your light. In imitation
of the shifting prism,
the hostility,
of another life.

The city cascading down; people churning like stones in a plunge pool; tall buildings with glass facades.

Zach has been here for years. I notice the nonchalance with which he handles everything: never lost on the subway or confused on the streets, gliding gently through the cacophony.

The man on the sidewalk pissing into a honey bear is nothing to Zach. His gait is immaculate.

I decide to emulate my friend one step at a time; I resolve to walk with confidence through the crowds before taking on bigger challenges.

I practice daily. Deep breaths in the apartment doorway. Wear through a pair of Converse in no time.

Then I am running panicked through the traffic: the cars are bulls around me. I bump into everyone in Manhattan twice before my manners return.

I am exposed and around and alone: viscera everywhere like angry spaghetti. In Brooklyn I excuse myself to a telephone pole. Then I focus. Then I improve.

By late fall, Zach seems a timid child in traffic: crossing with the signals; hanging back, listening to the insects by the river with reverence.

He asks how I'm adjusting. I say I think I've gotten better at walking. What does he think? He shrugs his shoulders. He hasn't noticed my walking.

We look to the constant Hudson, not yet winter frozen, not yet tectonic with springtime, as I've heard happens.

I swallow blue fluid from a plastic bottle; my inner ear is muffled briefly by the action.

A party barge. Silent dancers. The sun on the river. I close my eyes.

Wind is the first thing I am aware of. As though I am standing at the entrance of a tunnel, the traffic returns first to my skin, then to my ears.

I apologize to nothing in particular. We continue to the top of Manhattan.

Train

A line of faces   strung parallel
by the train car   Flashing open
and shut   Tacking off the moments
with their eyes   going on for miles
In the window birds appear
confetti caught in the light between buildings
The sky is cold and blue   But the sagging rooftops
are every color you might imagine
Then I am home   I find paper
and lay the composite   blank beads
wrapped around brown Christmas trees
Paper moving up   Down
As if it mattered   The faces on a train
A building's slump   Hollow bird bones
Filling time   space   Shoulders jostling in unison
Eyes ahead   Until I get it right

Liminal Poem: Between Nut and Tree

Dear Tree,
I want to climb you but can't:
No one, no matter how crazy,
has reached to your top.
They want to know why.
Why would I want to do this?
Why climb a tree?
Why climb you, whose
acorns are the you you were
before your bark was revised
by the tattoo of a chimerical hand?
And the answer:
I don't know. Or, maybe,
because I am here,
you are there,
and I've nothing better
to do than return. Circle.
I am on the edge
of a clearing. Across a green gulf
you rise before the rising sun.
An omen. Or a past.

The translation of Anna Akhmatova's

Requiem
1935-1940

*No. Not under the vault of a foreign sky,
nor carried by a stranger's broad wings—
In that time I stood with my people,
there, in our gray and unfortunate land.*

—1961

Instead of a Preface

     In the terrifying years of Yezhovism I spent seventeen months in the prison lines of Leningrad. Somehow, at some point, someone "recognized" me.

     Then the woman standing behind me, her lips blue in the cold light, a fellow sleepwalker who had certainly never heard my name before, woke from her fetters and whispered in my ear (there, everyone spoke in a whisper):

     —And this? Can you describe *this*?

     And I said:

     —I can.

     Then something resembling a smile slipped across the apparition that only a moment before had been her face.

--Leningrad, 1 April 1957

Dedication

The mountains kneel before our tragedy,
the great river is silenced at its source.
But our sorrow cannot break the prison locks;
behind them, despair tunnels endlessly on.

Will the spring breeze caress your face?
Will the sunset gently reveal you?
Not us. Our prison stretches to the sea:
everywhere the scream of key on stone,
and the slogging stamp of soldiers' boots.

We rose, as if for early Mass, and trudged
amid the tombstones of our ruined capital,
to face each other, more lifeless than the dead;
the sun sank low, the Neva misted,
and hope's song came only on the wind.

The verdict…and she cries out,
suddenly alien, torn from the crowd,
as if life were ripped directly from her chest,
as if thrown to the floor, brutally, in haste.
But she continues…staggers on…alone…

Where are they now, my shadow friends
from those two years in hell?
What visions are theirs in the blind Siberian wind?
What do they see in the dim halo of the moon?
Will they hear this, my last farewell? My final greeting.

—March 1940

Prologue

Only a corpse could smile,
content, finally, to rest.
Leningrad was a broken arm
hanging neglected in a prison yard.
Mad from torture, contorted regiments
marched around the prison's naked walls
while farewell songs wailed
from train horns.
Stars of death stood above us
as innocent Russia cringed
beneath bloody boots
and the tire tread of Black Marias.

I

They took you at dawn.
I followed, as if in a funeral procession.
In the dark pantry, children cried.
Before the Virgin Mother, a candle
  drowned in its own wax.
Your lips were chill from the icon's kiss.
The death-sweat on your brow…indelible.
Like the wives of Imperial Archers
I shall stand howling under the Kremlin's towers.

—1935

II

Quietly flows the quiet Don;
into my house slips the yellow moon.

He enters with his hat askew,
sees his shadow, that yellow moon.

This woman is sick to the bone,
this woman is sick and alone:

her husband dead, son shackled away.
Pray for me … for me, pray.

III

No. It is someone else who suffers.
I could not bear such pain. It isn't me.
Shroud it in black; have the moon eclipse it.
Let them carry the torches away …
                      Night.

IV

If I showed you, you silly girl,
beloved prankster, my merry
little sinner from Tzarskoye Selo,
what will happen to your life—
How you will stand, three-hundredth in line,
below rows of cruciate stone,
clutching a meager parcel, on New Year's ice
pockmarked by your tears.
See yourself at that silent dance, fixed
amid the sway of prison poplars. No sound.
No sound. Yet how many innocent lives
                              are ending. …

V

Seventeen months I have screamed,
calling you home to me.
I threw myself at your executioner's feet,
my son, my fate, my horror.
This moment is an infinite puzzle,
without solution, no, never for me:
man and beast, indistinguishable, crawling.

How long will I await this execution?

Only dusty flowers remain,
and the quiet thurible, smoking;
and footprints that lead to nothing.
The immense star looks into my eyes
threatening, threatening: a promise
of ready death.

VI

Time flies on, nearly weightless;
what happened, I don't understand.
This city's white nights peered
in on your prison cell; O, how again they watch
with a hawk's burning eyes: pale nights
speaking of death.

VII

The Sentence

And the stone word fell
on my still living breast.
It is all right. I was ready for this,
after all. I'll get by. Somehow …

I have the distraction of my chores:
I must destroy my past. Finally.
I must petrify my soul, then somehow
learn to nurture what remains—

Be that as it may … summer rustles
like a celebration outside my window.
I could smell it coming on the wind:
This sunny day; this empty house.

   —Summer, 1939

VIII

To Death

You will come in any case –why not now?
I am waiting for you –I cannot take much more.

I turned off the light and opened the door
for you. For you, so simple. And so strange.

Come to me, take any form you please:
burst through me like deadly hail;

strike me from behind like a weary thief;
fill my lungs, let me choke on your typhus gas.

Or recite the fairytale you concocted: That little story
which makes us all sick; your mouthful of churned vomit—

so again I see the top of a policeman's blue hat
and the caretaker, pale and trembling with fear.

It makes no difference. The Yenisei roils,
the North star shines, and they will not cease today.

But the last horror is setting
in my beloved's sea-blue eyes.

>   —The House on Fontanka St,
>   19 August 1939

IX

Already the wing of madness
has shadowed half my soul,
held fiery wine to my lips,
and drawn me into its black valley.

I knew that to this devil's wisdom
I must acquiesce: with tired ears
I listened to my garbling tongue,
then translated my own voice.

It says I may not take anything
along on my journey
(no matter that I politely ask
...no matter that I grovel)—

Not the fear of my son's face—
his paralyzed suffering— not
the day of that thunderous word,
nor the hour I met him in shackles.

Not his dear, cool hands,
nor a linden's restless shadow
touched by the murmuring wind,
nor his final words of consolation.

> —The House on Fontanka St,
> 4 May 1939

X

Crucifixion

> "Don't cry for me, Mother.
> Can't you see I'm in the grave?"

I

A choir of angels glorified the hour,
the gray sky turned to molten light.
"Father, why hast thou forsaken Me?
Oh, Mother, please don't cry for Me."

II

Mary Magdalene tore at her breast, sobbing;
the beloved disciple watched Him, petrified.
His Mother stood away from them, immersed
in her own silence, where no one dared glance.

—1940-1943

Epilogue

I

I learned how faces collapse under the weight
of a century, how terror peeks out from eyelids
cracked like stone tablets, and cuneiform suffering
etches its stony language on hollowed cheeks.
How a lock of cherished hair may turn
from black and gold, to hasty silver;
how smiles wither on resigned lips,
and terror becomes trembling laughter.
I'm not praying for myself alone,
but for everyone who stood there with me
in crippling frost, and in July's gnawing heat
before that blind red wall.

II

Again, the hour of remembrance draws near.
I see, I hear, I feel you; and I know them:

the fragile one we helped to the window,
the one who no longer wakes to her mother-

land; and the girl who shook her beautiful hair,
saying, "I have come." As if returning home.

I want to call out to them, each by name,
but the list that names them was stolen.

For them I weave a wide cloak
of shabby, eavesdropped words.

I remember them everywhere, always,
even in new troubles they are with me.

One hundred million people scream through
me, and if my tormented mouth is muzzled,

let them remember me as well, in my pen-
ultimate moment, on my own remembrance day.

And if, by chance, this country should one
day decide to erect a monument to me, well

I graciously grant my permission.
But on these conditions: do not place

it by the sea, where I was born:
the sea no longer touches me;

nor plant it in the Tzarskoy garden, near
the sacred stump, where shades hunt me out;

but place it here, where I stood for three hundred
hours. Here, where the prison door will not unbolt

for me. Because I dread a peaceful death— for fear
I might forget the thunderous charge of Black Marias,

forget the arrhythmic drumming of fists on a door,
or the wounded howl of the old woman behind it.

So let the melting snow stream like tears
from the forged bronze eyes of my colossus,

while a prison dove coos from afar,
and ships glide silently along the Neva.

      —March 1940

Шестое чувство

*a translation of Percy Bysshe Shelley's
"Ozymandias" from English into Russian*

Прекрасно в нас влюбленное вино
И добрый хлеб, что в печь для нас садится,
И женщина, которою дано,
Сперва измучившись, нам насладиться.

Но что нам делать с розовой зарей
Над холодеющими небесами,
Где тишина и неземной покой,
Что делать нам с бессмертными стихами?

Ни съесть, ни выпить, ни поцеловать.
Мгновение бежит неудержимо,
И мы ломаем руки, но опять
Осуждены идти всё мимо, мимо.

Как мальчик, игры позабыв свои,
Следит порой за девичьим купаньем
И, ничего не зная о любви,
Всё ж мучится таинственным желаньем,

Как некогда в разросшихся хвощах
Ревела от сознания бессилья
Тварь скользкая, почуя на плечах
Еще не появившиеся крылья,

Так век за веком — скоро ли, Господь? —
Под скальпелем природы и искусства,
Кричит наш дух, изнемогает плоть,
Рождая орган для шестого чувства.

Ozymandias

*a "Google Translation" of Percy Bysshe Shelley's
"Ozymandias" from English to Russian*

Я встретил путешественника из старинной земле
Кто сказал: <Две огромные и trunkless ногами камень
Встаньте в пустыне. Рядом с ними, на песке,
Половина затонул, разрушенной лицо лежит, чей хмурый взгляд,
И морщинистые губы, и насмешка холодного команды
Скажите, что его скульптор и те страсти читать
Какие еще выжить, печать на этих безжизненных вещей,
Стороны, которые насмехались над ним и сердце, что кормили.
И на пьедестале эти слова появляются –
"Меня зовут Ozymandias, царь царей:
Посмотрите на мои работы, вы крепкий и отчаяние! "
Ничего кроме останков. Вокруг распад
Из этого колоссальное крушение, безграничная и голые
Одинокий и уровень пески простираются далеко.>

The Sixth Sense

a translation of Nicolay Gumilev

How splendid that wine is our true love,
warm bread kindly bears our oven,
and woman's whisper plays in our ear:
her delicate gift of torment and pleasure.

But what do we do with the rosy dawn?
Her cool fingers glide through cloud,
where the sky meets calm mountains. …
And what do we do with immortal poems?

They are not ours to eat, drink, or kiss.
Their instant runs unstoppable, stampedes us,
and we break our hands, but are cursed
always to be swept onward: away and past.

We are like a boy, who has forgotten
youthful games, watching girls swim:
in ignorance of love, yet afflicted,
he suffers some numinous desire.

Once, amid the horsetails of a bog,
a slippery creature cried out
upon seizing its own impotence, as wings
bowed the skin beneath its shoulders.

— How soon, God?— Century after century,
under the blade of nature and art,
our spirit howls, our flesh labors,
giving birth to the organ of our sixth sense.

Giraffe

a translation of Nicolay Gumilev

Today, I see your gaze is particularly sad
and how your thin hands hug your knees.
But listen: far away on the banks of Lake Chad
wanders a marvelous giraffe.

He is a dancer, and his fleet body
is painted in mysterious patterns,
with which only the lake moon dares compete:
its silvery shattering of mirror and mist.

From afar he could be colorful ship sails in wind,
and his body flies through the sky like a bird.
Yes, I know this world is made of wonders,
when at sunset he hides in his marble grotto.

I know cheerful fairytales of strange countries
of the black maiden, and a young leader's desire,
but you've breathed the heavy fog for too long,
and you wont believe in anything but the rain.

So how can I tell you about tropical gardens,
slender palms, or the scent of unimaginable savannah.
You're crying? Listen … far away on Lake Chad
wanders a marvelous giraffe.

Two Jealousy Poems

On the Dangers of Reading Living Poets More Talented than Oneself

Reading Sarah Manguso on the train
and I am idiot-grin charmed when
I realize she is looking at me, a deer's
eyes blinking over the leaves of *Siste Viator*.

My stop. I pass, look from her to the book,
say, how nice and depart. Feel classy.
She has seen me: later, reading a new poem,
I see myself again saying how nice,
though made different somehow,

slightly more, and slightly less, myself.

Right now I regret
everything
I've ever done.

I Am Smoking Cigarettes Again

my arms on the window sill   the smoke
trailing back inside   My neighbor
is in the garden on her phone   A transparent moth
looks through the downstairs window

Between breaths I read Craig Arnold
who   for the five minutes I knew him
seemed so sincere   smiled when told
how I'd loved his book

Forever is an awfully long time
Forever   Craig Arnold is trapped in a volcano

Let's consider the use
of the second person
address in "Asunder"

                Today   I miss you terribly

Acknowledgments by Editors Kimiko Hahn and Rajiv Mohabir

Thanks to the editors of the following journals who understood our need to place these poems quickly: *The Kenyon Review, Plume, Storyscape,* and *Drunken Boat.*

And special thanks to the editorial board at Hanging Loose Press—in particular the Brooklyn contingent, Robert Hershon and Donna Brook.

Thanks also to the Queens College Foundation for their continued support.

***

A number of people participated in bringing this collection together—some while gathering poems for Hoyt's memorial. Special thanks to Jonathan Alexandratos, John Rice, Jason Fischedick and the writing collective *Oh, Bernice* for organizing the memorial reading.

Also, thanks to Jonathan Alexandratos for immediately starting a fund for what is now The Hoyt Jacobs Memorial Poetry Prize at Queens College; also, to John Rice and Jason Fischedick who worked with Jonathan on fundraising.

Thanks to his many other classmates who assisted in this posthumous project.

Thanks to his other poetry and translation professors: Susan Bernofsky, Nicole Cooley, and Roger Sedarat.

Thank you Olga Ardova who was co-translator for the poems from Russian and Hoyt's beloved friend.

Thank you to Hoyt's parents, Susan Posey and Bill Jacobs.

Hoyt Jacobs received his MFA in poetry and translation along with his MA in TESOL from Queens College, CUNY where he taught poetry and worked as an editor for *Ozone Park Journal*. Jacobs later worked as a reading and writing tutor at New York City College of Technology and was a member of the *Oh, Bernice!* writing collective. His work can be found in *The Kenyon Review, Plume, Storyscape Journal*, and other places. In January of 2015, an avid cyclist, Jacobs was struck and killed by a truck in Long Island City. He was thirty-six.